CALLING DR. WHOOPEE!

Doonesbury books by G. B. Trudeau

Still a Few Bugs in the System
The President Is a Lot Smarter Than You Think
But This War Had Such Promise
Call Me When You Find America
Guilty, Guilty, Guilty!
"What Do We Have for the Witnesses, Johnnie?"
Dare To Be Great, Ms. Caucus
Wouldn't a Gremlin Have Been More Sensible?
"Speaking of Inalienable Rights, Amy..."
You're Never Too Old for Nuts and Berries
An Especially Tricky People
As the Kid Goes for Broke
Stalking the Perfect Tan
"Any Grooming Hints for Your Fans, Rollie?"
But the Pension Fund Was Just Sitting There
We're Not Out of the Woods Yet
A Tad Overweight, but Violet Eyes to Die For
And That's My Final Offer!
He's Never Heard of You, Either
In Search of Reagan's Brain
Ask for May, Settle for June
Unfortunately, She Was Also Wired for Sound
The Wreck of the "Rusty Nail"
You Give Great Meeting, Sid
Doonesbury: A Musical Comedy
Check Your Egos at the Door
That's *Doctor* Sinatra, You Little Bimbo!
Death of a Party Animal
Downtown Doonesbury
Calling Dr. Whoopee

In Large Format

The Doonesbury Chronicles
Doonesbury's Greatest Hits
The People's Doonesbury
Doonesbury Dossier: The Reagan Years
Doonesbury Deluxe: Selected Glances Askance

A DOONESBURY BOOK BY
G.B. Trudeau

CALLING DR. WHOOPEE!

AN OWL BOOK · HENRY HOLT AND COMPANY · NEW YORK

To T-Bird

Published by Henry Holt and Company, Inc.,
521 Fifth Avenue, New York, New York 10175.
Published in Canada by Fitzhenry & Whiteside Limited,
195 Allstate Parkway, Markham,
Ontario L3R 4T8.

Library of Congress Catalog Card Number: 87-81346
ISBN 0-8050-0642-7

First Edition

Printed in the United States of America

The cartoons in this book have appeared in newspapers
in the United States and abroad under the auspices
of Universal Press Syndicate.

1 3 5 7 9 10 8 6 4 2

ISBN 0-8050-0642-7

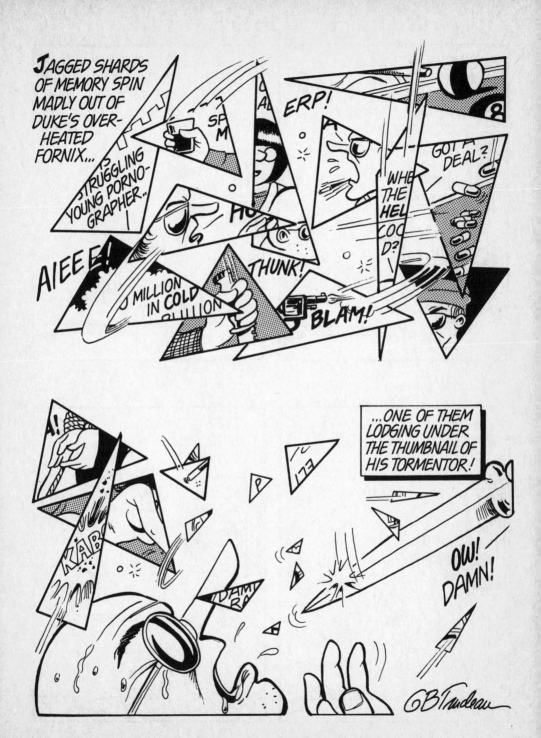

IS OUR CURRENT REPRESENTATIVE DRUG-FREE? UNLIKE HER CHALLENGER, MRS. DAVENPORT SAYS IT'S NONE OF OUR BUSINESS.

CLYDE

DAVENPORT

WHAT'S LACEY DAVENPORT HIDING? THE FOLLOWING VIDEOTAPE SUGGESTS ONE POSSIBLE EXPLANATION.

THIS IS OUR CONGRESSWOMAN IN A COMMITTEE HEARING LAST SUMMER, CLEARLY "NODDING OFF" DURING TESTIMONY!

GB Trudeau

THAT'S **SOUTH** OF THE **SUSPENDERS,** MISTER!

GEORGE SHULTZ WAS TESTIFYING, FOR HEAVEN'S SAKE!

WE STILL HAVE A PROBLEM, BOSS.

OKAY, WE OPEN WITH A KIND OF SCRAPBOOK, UNDERSCORING YOUR STRAIGHT-LACED, VICTORIAN UPBRINGING, ETC...

V.O. Back in 1912...

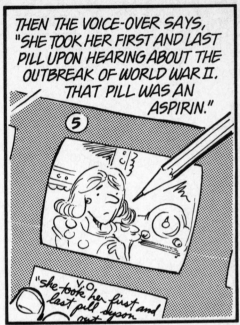

THEN THE VOICE-OVER SAYS, "SHE TOOK HER FIRST AND LAST PILL UPON HEARING ABOUT THE OUTBREAK OF WORLD WAR II. THAT PILL WAS AN ASPIRIN."

V.O. "she took her first and last pill upon..."

...THEN THE ANNOUNCER DROPS HIS VOICE A LITTLE AND INTONES, "DAVENPORT. CLEAN SINCE 1939." FADE OUT. LIKE IT?

DAVENPORT. Clean Since 1939.

V.O.

IT MAKES IT SOUND LIKE I DIDN'T TAKE A BATH DURING THE DEPRESSION.

HMM...

COULD YOU SOFTEN IT A LITTLE, MIKE?

GB Trudeau

WHEN ONE THINKS OF RICHARD WINDAMERE DAVENPORT, ONE THINKS OF A MAN WHOSE NAME WAS ALMOST SYNONYMOUS WITH THE BUFF-BREASTED FLYCATCHER.

WHY? WHY NOT BENDIRE'S THRASHER OR THE BRISTLE-THIGHED CURLEW? GOOD QUESTION. I RANG UP DICK'S SCHOOLMATE CECIL TO SEE IF *HE* KNEW, BUT HE WAS OUT WEEDING.

VINTAGE CECIL! IF IT'S NOT ONE THING WITH HIM, CHANCES ARE VERY GOOD INDEED IT'S ANOTHER. THE STORIES I COULD TELL YOU ABOUT THAT CHARACTER!

BUT I DIGRESS...

NOT AT ALL! CARRY ON, OLD BOY!

YES, TELL, TELL!

GBTrudeau

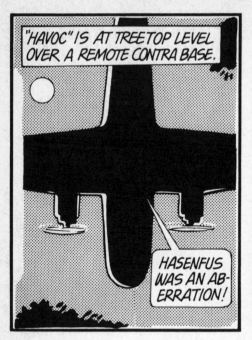

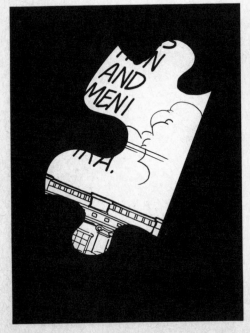

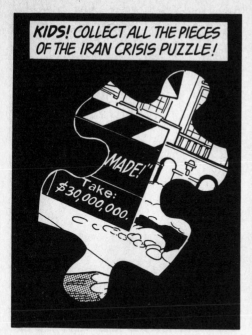

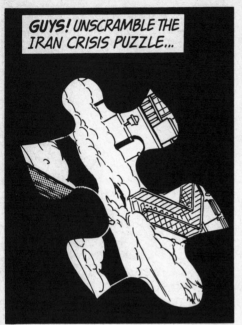

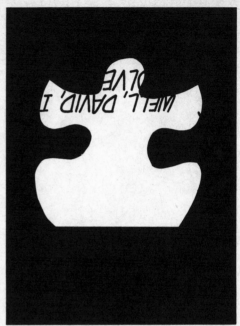

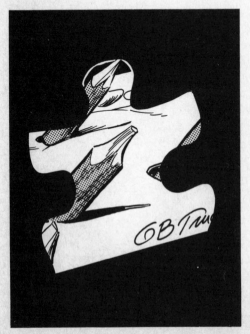

WELCOME BACK TO DAY 32 OF THE ORAL ROBERTS DEATH WATCH! MY PRODUCER JAKE AND I ARE STILL TALKING ABOUT GOD'S EXTRAORDINARY $4.5 MILLION SHAKEDOWN.

JAKE, I THINK WHAT CONCERNS ME MOST IS THE CLAIM THAT GOD IS HOLDING A LIFE HOSTAGE FOR FUND-RAISING PURPOSES, THAT HE IS, IN EFFECT, A COMMON TERRORIST.

AS ONE OBSERVER HAS PUT IT, "NO CAUSE CAN JUSTIFY TERRORISM. IT IS THE CRIME OF COWARDS. TERRORISM IS HEINOUS AND INTOLERABLE!"

WHO SAID THAT?

RONALD REAGAN.

STRONG STUFF. BUT WOULDN'T GOD KNOW HE DOESN'T MEAN IT?

©B. Trudeau

OKAY, WE OPEN ON A COUPLE OF Y-PEOPLE READING THE SUNDAY PAPER IN THEIR DUPLEX...

TITLE: "SAFE WHOOPEE"

Young couple in their apartment.

THEY LOOK UP AT THE SAME TIME AND EXCHANGE KNOWING, ROMANTIC GLANCES...

Exchange glan—

AS HE GETS UP TO DIM THE LIGHTS, SHE SAYS, "DARLING, LET'S BE SURE TO USE A CONDOMINIUM!" CUT TO PRODUCT NAME AND OUT!

he: "Hav—

WHAT DO YOU THINK?

NOT BELIEVABLE.

YEAH, YUPS SCHEDULE **EVERYTHING.**

GB Trudeau

GOOD EVENING. FOR FOUR MONTHS NOW, WASHINGTON HAS BEEN MESMERIZED BY THE PRESIDENT'S EFFORTS TO REMEMBER HIS ROLE IN THE IRANIAN AFFAIR.

CAN THESE MEMORIES EVER BE RETRIEVED? DO THEY IN FACT EXIST? FOLLOW ALONG AS WE TRY TO BRING 'EM BACK ALIVE IN...

L. DUCK

THE RETURN TO REAGAN'S BRAIN!

WHO? WHAT? WHEN?

THWITT!

MARCH 24, 1987—IT'S BEEN SEVEN YEARS SINCE MY LAST TREK THROUGH REAGAN'S BRAIN...

WHAT A BLEAK, RAVAGED LANDSCAPE GREETS US. CRANIAL COILS LAY HEAPED IN LIFELESS DISARRAY.

NEURONS ARE STRETCHED AND FRAYED, THEIR DENDRITIC SPINES WORN AWAY.

IN SHORT, NOTHING HAS CHANGED.

SEE? MY INITIALS!

RBH '80

GB Trudeau

MARCH 25 — PROGRESS UP THE BRAIN STEM IS MADDENINGLY SLOW. SLUDGE SLIDES BLOCK OUR WAY AT EVERY TURN.

FINALLY, WE GAIN A MESA OVERLOOKING A SWELTERING MASS OF NEURONS.

SHERPA!

SIRE?

WHAT PLACE IS THIS?

IT IS KNOWN AS THE CEREBRUM, SAHIB. IT IS WHERE THE PRESIDENT DOES ALL HIS CRITICAL THINKING.

SOUNDS PEACEFUL ENOUGH.

SHOULD WE SET UP THE BASE CAMP, SAHIB?

©B Trudeau

MARCH 31, 1987 — I AM KNOCKED SENSELESS BY THE PRESIDENT'S ATTEMPT TO HOLD TWO THOUGHTS SIMULTANEOUSLY. WHEN I AWAKE, SOMETHING CATCHES MY EYE.

WHY... IT'S A PRESS TAG!

ALARMED, I GLANCE ABOUT.

GASP!

I HAVE FOUND THE REMAINS OF ED GRANGER, THE RESPECTED A.P. RE-PORTER WHO DISAPPEARED DURING THE 1966 GUBERNATORIAL RACE!

I BURY HIM IN THE INNER EAR.

I'M NOT MUCH GOOD WITH WORDS, LORD...

APRIL 1— I PUSH ON. REAGAN'S MEMORY OF IRAN-GATE HAS BECOME MY HOLY GRAIL. BUT PROVISIONS SPENT, I GROW FAINT FROM HUNGER.

I RECALL SOMETHING MY SHERPA SAID ABOUT THE MICRO-ORGANISMS FOUND IN THE CRANIUM BEING HIGH IN PROTEIN.

I EAT MY BELT.